To my parents who told me I could do anything I wanted and

my husband, who believed in me when I did. - M.L.F.

The
Hopeful
Hodag

By Mary Lee Flannigan

Illustrated By T.L.Derby

To my best friend Shannon. We are

thankful for you always being there

for us. - T.L.D.

MacLaren-Cochrane Publishing, Inc.

Text©2021 Mary Lee Flannigan
Cover and Interior Art©2021 TL Derby

The Hopeful Hodag Dyslexic Edition

Library of Congress Control Number: 2021935600

First Edition

ISBN
Hardcover: 978-1-64372-399-0
Softcover: 978-1-64372-400-3

For orders, visit

www.MCP-Store.com
www.maclaren-cochranepublishing.com
www.facebook.com/maclaren-cochranepublishing

In the thick of the woods,
by a dark swampy lake.
Hodag wakes up
with a yawn and a shake.

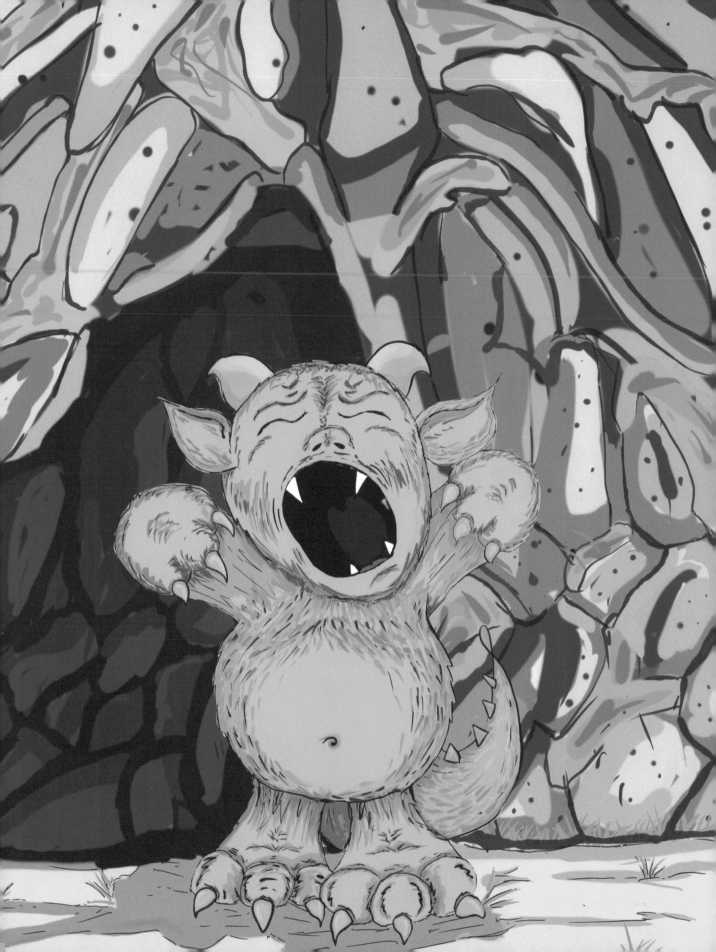

But Hodag is sad.
He's alone every day.
He's too scary and big,
and no one will play.

"They're afraid of my horns,
and my fangs and my claws.

"What I need is a friend, who
won't think these are flaws."

He takes off down the trail
by the crooked old trees.
With a chirp and a trill,
Chipmunk hops in the breeze.

By the path, near the leaves,
he hears a small smack.
A hedgehog is there,
by himself with a snack.

They give friendship a
try, Hodag and Skunk.
Two courageous new pals,
by the twisted tree trunk.

"Let's play hide and go creep,"
says Skunk with a grin.
Hodag hides by a bush,
trying to look small and thin.

Skunk scampers and snoops
over rocks, 'round the trees.
Soon he shouts, "I found you!"
And they laugh 'til they wheeze.

No more sadness for him,
Hodag has a new friend.
No long days all alone —
that has come to an end.

Mary Lee Flannigan - Author

As an artist, I hope my work will make children dream, explore, laugh, and be entertained. My favorite works are ones that take the reader on a journey, away from their everyday lives, and make them feel wonderful once they return. MaryLee lives with her husband Brad on Okauchee Lake in Oconomowoc, Wisconsin. They have 2 sons and a little 3-pound dog named Bear. When not writing, MaryLee can be found reading, exercising, and having adventures. MaryLee is the creator of the Lifesaver Ducks which are enjoyed by over 5 million children.

T.L. Derby - Ilustrator

T.L. Derby is a children's book author and Illustrator. She has turned her love for writing and art into her career. Now she helps others to make their dreams come true as a publisher. She is educated with a BFA in Creative Writing for Entertainment and an MFA in Creative Writing. She is also an autodidact in illustrating, screenwriting, and painting for over 20 years. Her love for children makes what she does a gift from her to the world.

What is Dyslexie Font?

Each letter is given its own identity making it easier for people with dyslexia to be more successful at reading.

The Dyslexie font:
1 Makes letters easier to distinguish
2 Offers more ease, regularity and joy in reading
3 Enables you to read with less effort
4 Gives your self-esteem a boost
5 Can be used anywhere, anytime and on (almost) every device
6 Does not require additional software or programs
7 Offers the simplest and most effective reading support

The Dyslexie font is specially designed for people with dyslexia, in order to make reading easier – and more fun. During the design process, all basic typography rules and standards were ignored. Readability and specific characteristics of dyslexia are used as guidelines for the design.

Graphic designer Christian Boer created a dyslexic-friendly font to make reading easier for people with dyslexia, like himself.

"Traditional fonts are designed solely from an aesthetic point of view," Boer writes on his website, "which means they often have characteristics that make characters difficult to recognize for people with dyslexia. Oftentimes, the letters of a word are confused, turned around or jumbled up because they look too similar."

Designed to make reading clearer and more enjoyable for people with dyslexia, Dyslexie uses heavy base lines, alternating stick and tail lengths, larger openings, and semicursive slants to ensure that each character has a unique and more easily recognizable form.

Our books are not just for children to enjoy, they are also for adults who have dyslexia who want the experience of reading to the children in their lives.

Learn more and get the font for your digital devices at
www.dyslexiefont.com

Get books in Dyslexie Font at: www.mcp-store.com

3	Hold my Hand	Short sentences, familiar words, and simple concepts for children eager to read on their own but still need help.